# Adventures in Writing for Children
## — Aaron Shepard —

Fifteen years after publishing *The Business of Writing for Children*—the all-time online bestseller among guides to children's writing—award-winning author Aaron Shepard returns with a new collection of articles on the art and business of creating literature for young people.

Topics include managing time in stories, structuring a chapter book, retelling folktales and legends, obtaining permissions, databases and business forms for children's writers, performance tips for author readings, online interaction with young readers, reviving a book with print on demand, converting from picture book to ebook, and more.

Whether you're aiming at traditional publishers or choosing to self publish, let *Adventures in Writing for Children* help you pursue an adventure of your own.

**Aaron Shepard** is the author of *The Legend of Lightning Larry*, *The Baker's Dozen*, and sixteen more picture books and early readers, along with several chapter books for middle grades, extensive resources for storytelling and reader's theater, and a graphic novel. His publishers have included Atheneum, Scribners, Clarion, Lothrop, Dial, and Harper-Collins, as well as *Cricket* and Australia's *School Magazine*.

Aaron's work has been honored by the American Library Association, the National Council for the Social Studies, the American Folklore Society, The New York Public Library, and the Bank Street College of Education. He has been a judge for the Golden Kite Awards of the Society of Children's Book Writers and Illustrators.

Aaron lives in Friday Harbor, Washington, in the San Juan Islands, with his wife and fellow author, Anne L. Watson.

*Books by Aaron Shepard*

### Writing and Publishing

The Business of Writing for Children • Adventures in Writing for Children • Aiming at Amazon • POD for Profit • Perfect Pages • From Word to Kindle • Pictures on Kindle • HTML Fixes for Kindle

### Reader's Theater

Stories on Stage • Folktales on Stage • Readers on Stage

### Picture Books & Easy Readers

Savitri • The Legend of Lightning Larry • The Legend of Slappy Hooper • The Enchanted Storks • The Gifts of Wali Dad • The Maiden of Northland • Master Maid • The Crystal Heart • Forty Fortunes • The Magic Brocade • The Baker's Dozen • The Sea King's Daughter • Lady White Snake • Master Man • The Princess Mouse • King o' the Cats • One-Eye! Two-Eyes! Three-Eyes! • The Adventures of Mouse Deer • Christmas Truce

### Chapter Books

Timothy Tolliver and the Bully Basher • The Mountain of Marvels • The Songs of Power • The Magic Flyswatter • The Monkey King • The Man Who Sang to Ghosts • The Swan Knight

### Graphic Novels

Robin Hood (with Anne L. Watson)

# Adventures in Writing for Children

More Tips from an Award-Winning Author on the Art and Business of Writing Children's Books and Publishing Them

# By Aaron Shepard

Shepard Publications
Friday Harbor, Washington

Cover sketch by Toni Goffe, coloring by Angelo Lopez

**Library of Congress subject headings:**
Children's literature—Authorship
Books—Marketing
Self-publishing

Version 2.0

You have to write whichever book it is that wants to be written. And then, if it's going to be too difficult for grownups, you write it for children.

Madeleine L'Engle

It does not seem to me that I have the right to foist a story on people—most of whom are children who should be learning all the time—unless I am learning from it, too.

Diana Wynne Jones

If a book comes from the heart, it will contrive to reach other hearts.

Thomas Carlyle

I'm not writing to make anyone's children feel safe.

J. K. Rowling

# Contents

# Getting Started

My earlier book on children's writing, *The Business of Writing for Children*, was drawn mainly from two sources: handouts from the classes and workshops I used to give, and my articles for *Once Upon A Time* and the *SCBWI Bulletin* (earlier called the *SCBW Bulletin*)—the newsletter of the Society of Children's Book Writers and Illustrators.

In selecting the articles to include in that book, I tried to keep a balance among its main subject areas—writing, publishing, marketing—and to avoid domination by my personal specialties. I also chose to omit my more controversial articles, to make the book more generally accessible.

Naturally, these criteria left out a number of articles I considered valuable. I'm pleased to offer at least some of them now, in this second collection. I've also included later articles, with some brand new ones—some of which I've meant to write for years. (There's nothing like publishing a book to help you tie up loose ends.) And as an added treat, I've thrown in the children's writer quotations featured on my Web site.

I hope you enjoy this new book and find it helpful. And if you want to read the articles I left out *this* time, you can find them on my Kidwriting Page.

*Aaron Shepard*

# Please Note!

**Though comments on this book are welcome, Aaron regrets he cannot provide help individually to aspiring writers.**

# Real Time

Time. No one has enough of it, no one can stop it, no one can make it pass one bit faster.

Unless, of course, you're an author.

Literature, more than any other art form, offers its creator almost limitless mastery of time. It can be stretched, shrunk, or even rearranged, all to suit the needs of the story. But you have to recognize the *kinds* of time at work in a story, and then learn the tools for manipulating them.

One kind of time serves as part of the story's *setting*, determining *when* the story takes place. Each chapter or other story division has a starting point in time from which it progresses. This point can be vague or specific; it can also be relative to the time it follows or else absolute, standing on its own. Direction is another option—the new starting point can immediately follow the preceding time, or jump forward to a later one, or backward to an earlier one.

Whatever the author chooses, the time is commonly set by some kind of *time marker*—any phrase that establishes the time for the reader. And to avoid confusion and uncertainty, this marker should normally be placed right at the chapter beginning or soon after.

> On May 14, at 2:32 in the afternoon, Muriel Terwillicker made her way through the girls' locker room at West Hollow High.

"Hand me that trowel!" said Megan.

"Coming right up!" said Richard.

It was just two weeks since the ice cream shack had burned down, and already another building was rising in its place.

Once upon a time, there was a boy named Jack.

The marker can also be indirect, perhaps supplied by a dated element.

Helmut anxiously inspected his chain mail and armor. This was the day of the tournament!

Mirial was all ready to go when Jonwen arrived in his heli-car.

The absence of *any* marker indicates a generic "anytime," which in the reader's mind places it roughly in the present or shortly after the time of the previous scene. If that's not what you want, don't leave out the marker!

Time, when used as setting, is so bound up with the story's structure that we might call it *structural time*. But *within* each chapter or other division, another kind of time is working. This time has to do with the *flow* of the story—how fast or slow it moves. I call this kind *narrative time*.

There are three types of narrative time an author can use. The first is *condensed time*. Though you can easily jump to a later time by starting a new chapter or such, sometimes you want to get there without a sharp break, while narrating at least some of what happened in the interim. Condensed time lets you do that, by speeding up the action. On a video player, the equivalent would be Fast Forward.

Ariel could hardly wait for the class to end. The teacher droned on as the minute hand on the clock crept upward. *Nine fifty-seven. Nine fifty-eight. Nine fifty-nine.* At last the bell rang.

She had promised to call him back, but as Justin hung up the phone, he realized she hadn't said when. The minutes stretched into hours, then days, then weeks. It wasn't until Labor Day that Justin faced the truth.

"Okay, I'll tell you about it from the beginning." It took over an hour, but by the end of it, he knew as much as I did and was just as excited.

The opposite of condensed time is *expanded time*. With this, a scene goes into slow motion while the author provides more information than would otherwise fit. This is commonly used, for instance, to thoroughly explore a character's thoughts—thoughts that in real life might pass in a flash, most likely nonverbally.

"Would you like to get together tonight?"
　　Marcy thought of the poor way he had treated her in the past. She thought of his reputation at school. She thought of her parents' strictness. She thought of her best friend and her crush on him. She thought of the next day's test, which would decide if she could follow the career of her dreams.
　　"Sure," she said.

Expanded time might also accommodate a detailed description of something a character observes in just a moment.

"Son, this has been in the family for generations. It's time for you to have it."

Percy stared at the object his father held out. It was a little like a clock, and a little like a kitchen blender. Fuchsia polka dots contended with tangerine stripes. Some surfaces looked shiny, others looked furry. There was writing on it in a language Percy didn't recognize and wasn't sure he wanted to. It seemed to be bleeding.

"Thanks, Dad," he said.

The remaining type of narrative time is what I call *real time*. As opposed to a scene in condensed or expanded time, a scene in real time is presented to the reader *in the time it would take in real life*. Well, sort of, because dialogue in a story must always be more efficient than real-life conversation, with less repetition and fewer wasted words. And there's also the factor of reading speed, which the author does not control. But the scene gives the *impression* of playing out at a realistic pace.

Real time has an important advantage over both condensed and expanded time. With those other types, the reader is more likely to mentally step back and think, "This is a story device."

With real time, on the other hand, the flow of the story as written can more closely match the flow of the movie that the story projects onto the reader's imagination. When that happens, the words on the page become less distracting and can almost disappear, allowing the reader to become more and more absorbed in the mental movie. The reader may almost forget that he or she is reading at all and become "lost in the story." This is the ultimate reading experience, and the one you should aim to provide.

How can you achieve this? One key, of course, is dialogue. For real time, it must all be in the form of direct quotation—the kind within quote marks—as opposed to indirect—the kind without.

But dialogue by itself won't give you real time—at least not always. If you've ever listened to young people, or even older ones, reading aloud, you'll know they seldom know when to pause. Dialogue becomes an unbroken stream of words—not the way people talk at all.

For real time, then, you have to *force* the pauses. And you do that by inserting narration. For example, consider this intentionally halting conversation.

> "I don't know," she said slowly. "I'll have to think about it." She stared at her bitten fingernails while I held my breath. "Well, okay, but will you promise me one thing?"
>
> That surprised me, but I also knew I wasn't likely to refuse whatever she asked. "All right."
>
> She chewed her lip, and I could see this wasn't easy for her. Finally she sighed. "Just promise you'll water my plants."

For a faster pace, on the other hand, you would want to reduce or even omit narration.

> "Stop it!"
> "No!"
> "I said, stop it right now!"
> "Make me!"
> "Okay, you asked for it!"

For a scene that *varies* in pace, you would vary the amount of narration accordingly.

One thing that can get in the way of real time is attributions—the "he said" and "she said" tags that tell the reader who is speaking. Putting an attribution tag on each line of dialogue is like jumping up and down in front of the reader and yelling, "Hey, I'm the author, and you're reading a story!" That's the worst form of expanded time. It's best, then, to leave out or remove any tags you don't really need.

There are actually three reasons you might need or want to attribute. The first and most important, of course, is to identify who is speaking when it is otherwise not clear. But this is needed less often than many writers think. All sorts of other clues can give away the speaker's identity: who spoke last, a name or term of address within the speech, a characteristic figure of speech or way of talking, the content of the speech. And often, when there's no clue already, one can be easily added.

"Can I go, Mom?"

"I may be smaller than you, but I'm smarter!"

"Leaping lizards!"

The clue can even be in accompanying narration, especially if the narration and dialogue are included in the same paragraph.

While the other students squirmed, Hilary raised her hand and waved it. "Teacher, teacher, call on me!"

My own rule when writing is to read through my dialogue, top to bottom, and for each speech ask myself if there can be any question about who is speaking. If there can be, I make sure there's a tag. If the speaker's identity is otherwise clear—and if I haven't added a tag for a different reason—I make sure there's none.

When tagging for identity, it's important that the tag be placed early in the paragraph—generally no later than at the end of the first full sentence. Remember there's a movie playing in the reader's mind. In the movie, that piece of dialogue will lack a voice and mouth for as long as the speaker's identity is unknown. If that goes on for several sentences, the movie sputters to a halt, and your reader is thrown out of real time.

The second reason to attribute is to append information on *how* something is said.

"And your mother too," he said jokingly.

"It's true," I said, with no hint of my uncertainty.

The third reason to attribute is to add a pause, as in our earlier example of real-time dialogue. But whether or not that's your purpose, any tag you add should be placed where a pause, however slight, might naturally occur.

"Well," said Maureen, "you might as well get it over with."

"That's one way to look at it," said Thomas. "But I see it a different way."

In regard to tags, there's one trap you should take care to avoid. Often writers are advised to avoid repeating the word "said" by substituting other verbs where possible. But the word "said," because of its shortness, simplicity, and the very repetition you're advised to avoid, is almost invisible to readers. This is not as true of any substitute.

Sometimes you *need* a different word, as when the speaker yells, cries out, whispers, pleads, or whines. But whenever a simple, solitary "said" will do the job, it's best to stick to that.

And that includes for questions! Questions don't automatically require "ask" or any other special verb!

"What do you think of *that*?" said Marion.

Of course, my advice about "said" assumes you're already minimizing the number of tags in your dialogue. If you insist on tagging every speech, whether that's needed or not, then any and all tags will sound deadeningly repetitive, regardless of variation.

Though dialogue may benefit most from being in real time, straight action may be helped as well. Compare the following two passages for their ability to draw in the reader. The first is in condensed time.

> Jake knew the release for the hidden door was somewhere, but where? He tried the underside of the fireplace mantel, behind the hanging mirror, around the window frame. No luck.

Now the same scene, but closer to real time.

> Jake knew the release for the hidden door was somewhere. But where?
>
> The underside of the fireplace mantel? He ran his hand carefully along its surface, from one end to the other, feeling for the slightest bump or crack. There was none.
>
> Behind the hanging mirror? Pulling gently on the bottom edge, he swung the mirror away from the wall and inspected the space behind, even running his hand across it. But the wall was blank and smooth.

Around the window frame? Jake's fingers glided around the full perimeter—bottom, left, top, right. *Wait, was that . . . ?* No, just a rough spot in the varnish.

No luck.

Once you know how to write in real time, the question is, when should you? The answer is, whenever you can. Scenes in real time should be the basic building blocks of your story, with shorter passages of condensed and expanded time working to supplement and connect them.

Time can be used in many ways to build and enhance your story. But the more you can keep your story in real time, the more it can come alive.

# Break It Down, Build It Up

It's always good to know your weak points, and here's a big one of mine: making choices. Faced with an array of decent yet not quite compelling options, I'm likely to freeze up and choose none. It's not so much I'm afraid of making a *bad* choice. I'm afraid of not making the *best*.

You can imagine the problems this might cause in my personal life. But it affects my children's writing as well. It's one reason I've focused mostly on picture books. Within just a few pages, there are only so many forks in the road to deal with. It's also a reason I favor retellings. Though in many ways I make such stories my own, some basic choices have already been made.

So, what happens when a guy like me tries his hand at an original chapter book? Starting out, not much.

The idea for this book came to me already wrapped in a title: *Timothy Tolliver and the Bully Basher*. It was to be a humorous story about a young inventor and the robot he created to fight off bullies. Though it would be set in a modern elementary school, I would base it roughly on the story of the Golem, the clay superman of medieval Jewish lore.

So far, so good. But now I had to devise and select enough plot details to fill about fifty manuscript pages.

And I just couldn't do it.

It wasn't that I couldn't come up with things that could happen in the story. I could come up with lots. But I couldn't decide what to use or what direction to take. Which resulted in paralysis.

That is, until I came upon an extremely helpful book: *The Comic Toolbox*, by John Vorhaus. His book saved mine—or more precisely, his chapter 7, "The Comic Throughline." There he described a common *structure* found in stories, both comic and dramatic, with examples drawn mostly from movies and television. In doing that, he broke the typical plot into several distinct stages, each with its own function and dynamics.

What this did for *me* was to take one huge, amorphous problem and break it down into a series of much smaller, more manageable ones. Though completely flummoxed by the challenge of working out my plot as a whole, I found it much easier to choose story elements for each plot stage. I soon had an outline and was ready to write.

I'm not going to exactly describe Vorhaus's prescribed structure. For one thing, it wouldn't be nice of me to give away that much of his book, which is still available, and which I very much recommend. For another, I didn't use his structure exactly as he gave it.

So, here instead are the plot stages I defined after tinkering with Vorhaus's, plus the plot "points" that start or end them. You can call this the "Tolliver Throughline."

**1. Setup.** Introduction to the characters, the setting, and so on.

**2. Kickoff.** A point that initiates the story. It could be an opportunity, a discovery, a threat, or a decision.

**3. Progress.** Things look good. Whatever the protagonist is doing is working. (This stage may be brief or omitted.)

**4. Point of reversal.** Uh-oh. There are unforeseen consequences, a new opponent, or another unexpected development.

**5. Regress.** Things fall apart. The protagonist is in deeper and deeper trouble.

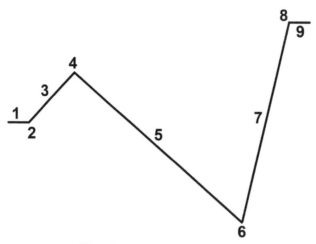

Plot Points and Stages

**6. Point of breakthrough.** Phew! The protagonist makes a discovery or a better decision, or has a bright idea or an important realization.

**7. Recovery.** Things come together. The protagonist is finally on the right track. (This stage may be brief or omitted.)

**8. Point of fulfillment.** Victory! A goal is reached, or a threat averted.

**9. Wrap-up.** Tying loose ends, saying good-bye.

Hanging my story elements onto this structure, here's the outline I came up with. Though I did make changes as I went along, the story stayed remarkably close to this.

---

Setup #1: Timothy and his friend Arnie are terrorized by gang of 6th graders.

Setup #2: Timothy shows Arnie a robot boy he's created for science fair. They get idea of using boy against bullies.

---

Progress #1: Try operating boy by remote control, but bullies easily get the better of him.

Progress #2: Bring boy to life by introducing YHVH into circuitry.

Progress #3: Boy takes on bullies and defeats them.

Regress #1: Timothy or sister try using boy for chore, but literal-mindedness causes problem. They discover he likes sister's flute.

Regress #2: Timothy brings him to school as cousin with speech problem. Boy attacks bullies at recess, who aren't doing anything.

Regress #3: Brought to principal's office, attacks principal. Runs amok and runs away.

Regress #4: Boy attacks bullies throughout town (as seen on TV news reports): Mom scolding kid, policeman handing out ticket, older brother picking on younger sister. Timothy realizes his only choice is to decommission the boy. Overcomes reluctance to admit his invention is no good and undo it. (It's his baby.) Calls gang to make deal, enlists sister.

Recovery: Deal is, will turn off boy if gang will help and also stop bullying. Gang acts as decoy. Sister's flute pacifies. Timothy removes YHVH from circuitry. Gang is impressed and respectful when they discover boy is a robot.

Wrap-Up: Timothy wins science fair for remote-controlled boy.

I wish I could report that *Timothy* was a huge success. Alas, I never found a publisher to buy it. Still, it did receive some nice comments from editors, and it also did moderately well when I later self published it. For these accomplishments, I thank John Vorhaus's structured approach to plotting.

Of course, this kind of approach isn't for everyone. In fact, I would be among the last to say you *should* write to *any* formula, much less a particular one. But if you find yourself, as I did, stymied by a breadth of choices, you too might find it helpful to break it down and build it up.

# The Art of Retelling

Folktales have been a mainstay of picture book publishing and hopefully always will be. Yet converting a folktale to a picture book story is tricky at best. The reteller must capably fill three distinct and often conflicting roles: Storyteller, Folklorist, and Author.

## Storyteller

The Storyteller understands and appreciates the world of the folktale. It is a world of external action and concrete symbol. The story is presented in bold strokes, with little descriptive detail, and language must be simple, direct, and lively. Characters seldom have names, but if they do, the names are the most common possible, or the most magical. Though the structure is sometimes complex, it is almost always linear: first this happened, then this, then this.

The Storyteller also knows that a folktale is not a static object, but an evolving and adapting organism. Most folktales can be found in different versions all over the world, because master storytellers have heard them from travelers and customized them for a home audience. Within a culture, too, a folktale has development. Passing from mouth to mouth, it deteriorates as details are forgotten or garbled. Yet sooner or later it is picked up by another master storyteller capable of recreating it.

---

Updated from the *SCBWI Bulletin,* June–July 1995.

It is the duty and joy of all Storytellers to improve a tale if they can, to pass it on better than they received it. It might mean the replacement of an obviously missing motif with one from a parallel version. Or the addition of a catchy phrase or verse. Or a magical name for the main character. Or a more satisfying ending. But when an enduring tale is made even stronger, there is cause for rejoicing in the worldwide family of Storytellers—past, present, and future.

## Folklorist

To the Storyteller, a folktale is universal and an end in itself. But to the Folklorist—as to the educators and librarians who are the main buyers of these books—a retelling is an opportunity to accurately represent and educate about another culture. So even as the Storyteller strives to lift a tale to a higher level, the Folklorist looks on sternly and says, "Mustn't stray too far! It's not your story!"

But the relationship is not entirely adversarial, because the methodical-minded Folklorist happily takes on the drudge work that holds little interest for the Storyteller. The Folklorist loves nothing better than to search library shelves, standard references, and online catalogs for the oldest and most authentic sources of folktales. Nor does the Folklorist mind the hours spent in the study of a culture to get all the details right.

It is one of the greatest joys of the Folklorist to produce a detailed author note on the sources and cultural context of the story—documentation increasingly demanded and scrutinized by educators and librarians. Here too the Folklorist helps the Storyteller. If the critical reader can be dazzled with thorough research and an extensive source listing, the Storyteller's alterations can more easily slip by.

## Author

Even as the Storyteller and the Folklorist bicker between themselves, both must deal also with the Author.

The Author says, "Folktale or not, it still has to meet the requirements of a picture book story! We'll have to shorten and simplify it. The violence must be toned down, and the sex will have to go. All right, the main character can be older than the reader, but he or she still has to solve the problem and grow as a result. The story must have a theme!"

Ah, yes, a theme. Picture book stories, like most fine modern literature, are driven by theme. Folktales, on the other hand, are driven by motif, and most have no theme whatever. Of course, this doesn't bother the Storyteller or the Folklorist. But the Author can't abide it, and neither can any English-major-turned-editor.

It is exactly here that the Author's most important contribution is made. Ignoring the protests of the Folklorist, the Author must sift the folktale, and from a hint here and a glimmer there, create a theme! And all at once, a loosely-related string of events becomes a unified story, a "slight" tale becomes a sellable manuscript.

So it goes: Storyteller, Folklorist, Author, all jockeying for position and protecting their turf. But if somehow they work out their differences and the tale emerges whole, then the Storyteller dances for joy, the Folklorist grins, and the Author sighs in relief.

The folktale is retold!

# Building a Legend

You would think there couldn't be two literary forms farther apart than a retold folktale and a feature article in a magazine. Yet, there is one place where these two might meet: in the Land of Legend. And when they do, children's magazines eat it up.

As a journalism student in college, one of the cardinal rules I heard was "Don't bury the lead." In newspaper articles, the lead—or *lede*, as it's pronounced and often spelled—is usually a brief statement of basic facts. But in magazine articles, it is more often a "soft lead"—a human-interest hook that draws the reader in while giving a good idea of what the article is about. After that, the writer can backtrack to fill in facts and provide context. But if you "bury the lead" by not starting with the hook, your reader may move on before they ever reach it.

Journalism turned out to be a bad match for me, and luckily, I discovered the gentler, more nurturing world of children's writing. Though my journalism training did carry over in helping me write more simply and economically, I could now set aside some other tools and rules I'd been given. For my folktale retellings and original fairy tales, I no longer had to handle hard-edged facts, like sharply defined whos, wheres, and whens. I also no longer needed to lead with the most interesting part of my story. I just started at the beginning and proceeded to the end.

But as I explored the world of folklore, one genre stood apart and seemed to invite a different treatment. *Legends*, I learned, were a type of folktale, but were linked to a specific person, place, and/or time.

These legends were *supposed* to be true—but usually were not. For one thing, the hero of the legend might never actually have lived! Or even if the person was real, the events of the legend might not have happened to him or her or anyone else.

In fact, over the centuries, the same legendary events might have migrated to a *series* of popular figures, real or mythical, as each new hero eclipsed the one before. Or the events might have crossed cultural borders to be linked to different heroes for different people. In a best-case scenario, both the person and the events were real and truly linked but had been . . . improved.

Don't think you know any legends of this kind? Then you probably do but don't realize it! For example, most Americans have heard legends about "Founding Father" George Washington—including his boyhood "I cannot tell a lie" about cutting down a cherry tree, or his throwing an anachronistic silver dollar across the mile-wide Potomac River.

That's right, those are total legends—or *apocryphal stories*, as legends are sometimes more stiffly called. The truth is, you can hardly look anywhere among stories of the past—of a nation or place or ethnic group or religion—without running into legend.

By the way, you may also know one kind of "legend" that is *not* a legend. That's a *tall tale*. Though they're often titled "The Legend of . . . ," the term is used there only whimsically and with tongue firmly in cheek. Everyone knows that a tall tale only *pretends* to be true. That's part of the fun. But with a real legend, you're sincerely asked to *believe*.

Besides the masquerade of fiction as fact, I discovered another important characteristic of legends: They're generally much simpler than other folktales, and often no more than an anecdote. As wonderful as many legends were to me, I found few with enough substance for a picture book. But by the same token, I thought some might be perfect for a children's magazine, which could welcome shorter pieces that fit between longer ones.

With this in mind, I started to think how to tailor such stories further to magazine readers. That's when my college training kicked in. The idea came to me that, with the strong, specific details in a legend, I could retell it in the form of a nonfiction magazine article—lead and all! Not only would the early hook help to draw in readers, but the unconventional structure would bring variety to the magazine's stories and make mine stand out.

I gave it a try, eventually applying the approach to three likely candidates from my research files: "The Harvest That Never Came," "The Most Precious Thing in the World," and "The Stone in the Temple." (Those are just my own titles for them!) To give you a better idea what I did, let's look at the first of them.

"The Harvest That Never Came" is from Sweden, about a prisoner of war who finds a way to return home and marry his childhood sweetheart. I found it in a favorite collection of public domain folklore retellings, Claire Booss's *Scandinavian Folk and Fairy Tales*, where it hid behind the much less attractive title "The Master of Ugerup." The legend is especially appealing, I think, because it has not only a peace theme but an ecological one as well. And though (*cough, cough*) the story *might* not be true, it *could* be—and at the least, it is told about real families and locales of the 1500s.

I could have started with a few sentences about how Danish noble Arild Ugerup grew up in Sweden, fell in love with Thale Thott, was later drafted into the Danish navy to fight Sweden, and was then captured by the Swedes—in other words, with a standard chronological beginning. And that beginning might easily have lost the reader, who could have been put off by the story's initial complexity.

Instead, I wrote a magazine-style lead.

*My dearest Arild,*

*I promised to wait for you forever, but I fear I will not be allowed to. My father says you will never return, and he has chosen another man to be my husband. Though I pleaded with him, he has already set the marriage date.*

*I will love you always.*

*Your faithful Thale*

Arild Ugerup, son of a noble Danish family, sat on his cot, reading the letter by the dim light of his prison cell. *How cruel the tricks played by war,* he thought, his eyes filling with tears.

Hooked yet? If so, I should be able to fill in the background without too much danger of losing you.

Though Arild and his family were nobles of Denmark, they had long lived peaceably in Sweden. When King Erik of Sweden was crowned, Arild had been one of his honored guests. But then Denmark and Sweden declared war on each other, and Arild was drafted into the Danish navy. He was captured in battle and imprisoned by King Erik.

Arild's childhood sweetheart, Thale Thott, had promised to marry him when he came back from the war. Now it seemed he would lose Thale as well as his freedom.

Which brings us back to where we left our hero, letting us pick up the thread.

Arild sat thinking for many hours, the letter lying loose in his hand. At last he crossed to a small table. Dipping his pen in an inkwell, he began to write.

*Your Royal Majesty,*

*Though I am now your prisoner, you once counted me as a friend. Grant me one favor. Let me go home to marry the woman I love. Then allow me to stay only long enough to plant a crop and harvest it.*
*On my word of honor, I will return to your prison as soon as the harvest is gathered.*

Of course, Arild comes up with a clever plan to keep his word yet stay with Thale, and the legend has a happy ending—but I wouldn't want to spoil it for you. Anyway, the solution is simple enough that it let me wrap up the story in just another two hundred words, bringing the total count to less than five hundred. One of the other legends I retold was twice as long, with nearly a thousand words, but the other was even shorter, with about 350. By contrast, most of my folktale retellings run closer to fifteen hundred!

Linus Pauling once said, "The best way to have a good idea is to have lots of ideas." Well, this certainly was one idea that made up for some of my others. Of the three legends I retold in this format, *all* were published in both *Cricket* magazine and Australia's *School Magazine*. (By comparison, my overall *Cricket* acceptance rate has been about one-third.) What's more, I sold each story three to five more times to inquiring textbook publishers and other rights buyers.

Could I have sold these legends with a more traditional structure? Quite likely. All were strong stories with attractive themes, and they did have the advantage of brevity. But I believe that the feature-article format moved them beyond being strong contenders to being nearly irresistible to a children's magazine editor.

And that is the stuff of legend.

# The Harvest That Never Came
## A Swedish Legend
## Retold by Aaron Shepard

*My dearest Arild,*

    *I promised to wait for you forever, but I fear I will not be allowed to. My father says you will never return, and he has chosen another man to be my husband. Though I pleaded with him, he has already set the marriage date.*
    *I will love you always.*

*Your faithful Thale*

Arild Ugerup, son of a noble Danish family, sat on his cot, reading the letter by the dim light of his prison cell. *How cruel the tricks played by war,* he thought, his eyes filling with tears.

Though Arild and his family were nobles of Denmark, they had long lived peaceably in Sweden. When King Erik of Sweden was crowned, Arild had been one of his honored guests. But then Denmark and Sweden declared war on each other, and Arild was drafted into the Danish navy. He was captured in battle and imprisoned by King Erik.

Arild's childhood sweetheart, Thale Thott, had promised to marry him when he came back from the war. Now it seemed he would lose Thale as well as his freedom.

Arild sat thinking for many hours, the letter lying loose in his hand. At last he crossed to a small table. Dipping his pen in an inkwell, he began to write.

*Your Royal Majesty,*

*Though I am now your prisoner, you once counted me as a friend. Grant me one favor. Let me go home to marry the woman I love. Then allow me to stay only long enough to plant a crop and harvest it.*

*On my word of honor, I will return to your prison as soon as the harvest is gathered.*

Arild signed and sealed the letter, then called the jailer.

The reply came the next day. King Erik had agreed! Arild was free—at least until the harvest.

Arild returned home, where Thale met him joyfully. Her father was not happy to have his plans changed, but in the end the two were married.

Now it was spring, the time for planting. And, in only a few months, Arild would have to harvest his crop and return to King Erik's prison.

Arild thought long and hard about what he would plant. At last he went to the fields and planted his seeds, placing each of them six paces from the rest.

Late that fall, a messenger arrived from King Erik. "The harvest season is past," he said. "The King awaits your return."

"But my crop is not harvested," said Arild. "In fact, it has not yet sprouted!"

"Not sprouted?" said the messenger. "What did you plant?"

"Pine trees," replied Arild.

When King Erik heard what Arild had done, he laughed and said, "A man like that does not deserve to be a prisoner."

Arild was allowed to remain home with his beloved Thale. And a magnificent forest stands today as a testament to his love.

# The Perils of Permissions

The use of quality children's literature in the classroom has been a boon to most authors, but there is one group it has seriously hurt: independent anthologists.

Why? With an increase in the demand for reprint rights, permissions fees have spiraled out of sight, and the terms of license have shrunk to as little as three years—or even one printing! Also, response times have lengthened to be often as ridiculous as those taken by editors to respond to manuscript submissions. As a result of all this, many worthwhile projects are now infeasible.

Some years ago, I had the pleasure and torment of producing a collection of reader's theater scripts called *Stories on Stage* (published by H. W. Wilson in 1993, and now in a second edition from Skyhook Press). Picture books, short stories, and novel extracts by contemporary authors were adapted into script form for use in middle-grade and junior-high classrooms, with the primary goal of promoting reading.

There was only one other such diverse collection of reader's theater scripts in print, and none for that age group. I soon discovered at least one reason why. The permissions quagmire is so frustrating and demanding, there are few authors who would have both the skill to produce the scripts *and* the fortitude to see them through publication.

Still, I was able to learn much that would be helpful to others in similar situations. Here are a few tips.

---

Updated from the *SCBWI Bulletin,* October–November 1994.

**Set a realistic permissions budget.** In 1992, the fee request for a picture book, short story, novel extract, or poem could easily reach $2,000, and sometimes higher. Based on such figures, a reasonable budget would allow *at least* $1,000 per piece as an average, and preferably $1500.

In general, permission fees are considered your responsibility. Sometimes a publisher will grant a permissions budget, or give an advance on royalties to go toward fees—but be aware that such a budget or advance may not cover your total costs, and may not be meant to do so. Children's anthology editing can become a form of subsidy publishing, and the benefits may be more professional than financial.

**Include all essential information with your permission requests.** The lack of a single item can create a delay of months. Include *all* of the following:

- Title of your book
- Author/editor (your name)
- Publisher
- Publication date
- Estimated page length of the book
- Total number of selections
- Binding (hardcover and/or paperback)
- Edition (trade or textbook)
- Estimated print run (number of copies)
- Estimated list price
- Identification of selection (title, author, chapter, etc.)
- Word count of the adaptation or reprint text
- Exact rights requested (reprint, North American, etc.)
- A request for a tax I.D. number—Federal I.D. or Social Security number, in the United States—for any payment to be administered by your publisher
- *A copy of your adaptation or reprint text*

# Aaron Shepard

P. O. Box 555          Hometown, California 55555 USA          555-555-5555

October 27, 1992

Dorothy Markinko
Macintosh & Otis
310 Madison Avenue
New York, NY 10017

Dear Ms. Markinko,

I am a freelance children's writer and performer, currently preparing a collection of reader's theater scripts for middle-grade and junior-high students. *Stories on Stage* will provide a key educational tool for a literature-based curriculum, as well as significant promotion for featured literature and authors.

Publication by H. W. Wilson is set for summer 1993, with a print run of 5000, in hardcover only. This book of 160-200 pages will be sold primarily to libraries at about $30.00. H. W. Wilson does not sell through trade book stores.

I request one-time world English-language rights to publish a reader's theater script adaptation of the following:
THE PUSHCART WAR, Jean Merrill, HarperCollins, 1992, foreword and chapters 1, 3-7. The approximate word count of the script adaptation is: 1800.

Please note that the rights I request fall under "reprints and adaptations" rather than dramatic rights. I do *not* request performance rights of any kind. Also please note that the entire permissions budget allowed by my publisher is $8000, which must pay for a minimum of 20 scripts. Please set your fee accordingly. Scripts that do not fit within this budget cannot be included.

A signature below will signify your permission. Please indicate any specific form of acknowledgement you require in the book. For payment, please include your Federal I.D. or Social Security number.

Thanks for your prompt action. If you do not entirely control these rights, *please* let me know quickly!


REQUIREMENTS:


SIGNATURE: _____

NAME (print): _____

DATE: _____

F.I.D./S.S.#: _____

## Sample Permissions Letter

If you are not sure of any of this information—especially the rights you need—consult your publisher. In fact, your publisher may draft a sample request for you or supply a standard one. But don't feel shy about adding any of these items if missing.

If you like, you can also offer a specific fee. This may discourage some higher fee requests, but it will also forestall lower ones. In any case, you may want to set any standard offer at a figure *below the average* you can pay, because some requests will surely be higher.

**Follow up within a couple of months.** Small projects often wind up at the bottom of big piles. Be persistent, but not obnoxious. Follow up by mail, or preferably by phone. If by mail, include a copy of your original request. If by phone, give the date of that request. Make careful notes of who you talk to and what is said.

**Negotiate the terms.** In most cases, fees are flexible, even if not as flexible as you'd like. I was able to get a number of fees lowered by one-third to one-half. One lovable permissions manager reduced her fees by two-thirds when I let her know I couldn't afford anything higher.

Take special note of the term of license, which can be five years or less. To avoid the hassle of renewal, you may sometimes find it worthwhile to negotiate a *higher* fee in exchange for a longer permission period.

Finally, note *when* the fee must be paid. If the contract specifies immediate or prompt payment after signing, this can sometimes be changed to payment on publication. This is safer, because you might wind up not using the piece—or your book itself might be postponed or canceled. (If a fee is due on publication and you don't use the piece, you don't have to pay.)

Jim Trelease recommends asking first for fee "estimates" or "quotes" instead of contracts. This way, you can make a final selection based on price before any payment is required.

**Have more material than you need.** Chances are, some permissions will fall outside your price range, even after negotiation, and others will be flatly denied. Always have enough selections so that some can come out. If you have to come up with new material and start the permissions cycle all over, your book will be drastically delayed.

**Don't take it personally.** Your project may be terribly important to you, but to the harried permissions manager who receives your request, it's just one of thousands. No matter how frustrating the process, maintain professionalism and courtesy. State your case clearly, and give the other person the opportunity to rethink and compromise. Even in the permissions quagmire, good communication skills can sometimes produce small miracles.

# Databases for the Children's Writer

Most writers who submit their work soon learn the importance of keeping detailed records. They find it's essential to record which manuscript has been sent to which editor at which publisher on what date and with what results. Usually, they keep this information on index cards or log sheets, one for each title.

The shortcoming of this method shows up after you've made many submissions of many titles and then need to cross-reference. Yes, you can easily see which publishers have considered a particular manuscript. But it's not so easy to see which manuscripts have gone to a particular publisher—and the more you submit, the harder it gets.

Of course, you could keep a separate set of records organized by publisher—but that complicates things considerably. And it still doesn't help in tasks like tracking submissions to a particular editor who has moved through several publishers.

The solution is a computer database. Once your records are in electronic form, you can easily search and sort by title, publisher, editor, or anything else you care about. In fact, you're sure to think up new questions to ask of your records. For instance, I can quickly tell you that my overall ratio of submissions to acceptances is . . . . Um, never mind.

For my own submissions database, I use FileMaker, which is available for both Mac and PC. Here are the fields I include:

---

Updated from the *SCBWI Bulletin,* March–April 2001.

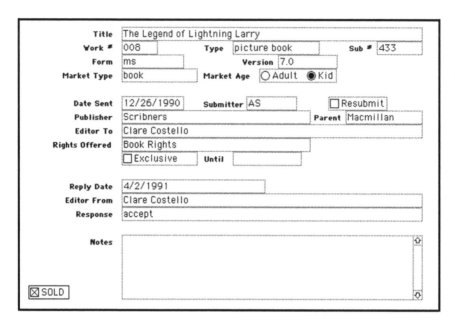

Submissions Database

**Title.** The title of the work.

**Work #.** This is a unique identifier for each work—for instance, A73 for this article. The identifier helps me keep track of a work if the title changes. Of course, I use the same identifier—along with title keywords—to label the work's folders on my computer and in my paper files.

**Work type.** The genre—picture book, easy reader, chapter/novel, nonfiction, or collection for book-type submissions; story, script, article, or poem for others. I select my choice from a pop-up list.

**Submission #.** A unique serial number for each database record, entered automatically by the program. This number helps me track the submission between this database and a related one for sales.

**Form.** The kind of material submitted—manuscript, query, proposal, or previously published book—all in a pop-up list.

**Version.** I put a version number on each of my manuscript and proposal drafts, numbering them like computer programs—1.0, 1.1, 2.0, and so on. Noting the version number in a submission record then lets me know exactly what I've sent. (My agent, though, tells me not to print the number on submission copies themselves.)

**Market type.** Book, periodical, anthology, theater, film/TV, Web, miscellaneous—all in a pop-up list.

**Market age.** Adult or kid, selected by radio buttons.

**Date sent.** The date in a sortable format.

**Submitter.** Either me, my agent, or both combined, in a pop-up list. (Though my agent handles submissions of most new book manuscripts, I commonly submit older ones, magazine stories, articles, and so on. I also keep records of her submissions so I can track my stories and make suggestions.)

**Resubmit?** A check box to tell if this is a repeat submission of this title to this editor and publisher.

**Publisher.** The one sent to. For a periodical, this is the publication name.

**Parent.** If the publisher is an imprint, I put here the publishing house it's part of. For a magazine, I put the magazine group—for instance, Cricket, for *Cricket* magazine and all its sister mags. A pop-up list provides names I use often.

**Editor to.** The editor addressed, if any.

**Rights offered.** Book, First Serial, Reprint, and so on, in a pop-up list.

**Exclusive?** A check box showing whether this is an exclusive submission.

**Until.** A cut-off date for exclusive consideration. (This date would be given to the editor on submission only. Generally, there is then no need to give later notice or to withdraw the manuscript before sending it elsewhere.)

**Reply date.** In a sortable format. I can quickly tell which submissions are still out by searching for "blanks" in this field.

**Editor from.** The editor replying, if a name is given. (This may not be the editor submitted to.)

**Response.** This pop-up list has all possible responses: accept, reject, conditional (on successful revision); lost, returned, withdrawn, replaced (by a later manuscript version); none, unknown; and—for queries and proposals—invite, decline, and postpone.

**Notes.** Explanations, editor comments, or anything else.

**Sold?** A checkbox for quick sorting and to tell me there's sales info in a related database.

To let you search and sort your records, you need to standardize how you enter much of your information. For instance, you don't want to use different forms of a publisher's name—like both "S&S" and "Simon & Schuster." You must also watch your spelling, as a single mistake can make a record invisible to a search.

These are the reasons I make liberal use of pop-up lists, radio buttons, and check boxes. (Pop-up lists—as opposed to pop-up menus—also let you type in text directly if none of the choices apply, or if more than one does.) If the program you're using doesn't offer such features, you might keep a "style sheet" handy, showing each common entry in the form you've settled on.

Also vital for any database: MAKE SURE YOU HAVE BACKUPS! Years of records could be corrupted or lost in a split second, so don't take chances. You should have a series of dated copies, with at least some away from your computer, and at least one away from your home.

Of course, once you start with databases, you're not likely to stop with recording just submissions. For instance, I use two separate databases to record sales. The book sales database has details of book contracts, such as which rights I've reserved. The story and article sales database holds info on magazine and similar fee-based sales, including whether I've been paid.

| | |
|---|---|
| **Title** | The Legend of Slappy Hooper |
| **Work #** | 009 **Type** story **Sub #** 136 **Piece Sale #** 3 |
| **Reprint From** | |
| | |
| **Sale Date** | 9/15/1989 **Negotiator** AS |
| **Buyer** | Cricket **Parent** Cricket |
| **Contact** | Lynn Gutknecht |
| **Market Type** | periodical **Market Age** ○ Adult ◉ Kid |
| | |
| **Rights Granted** | First North American Serial |
| **Restrictions** | |
| **Granted For** | |
| | |
| **Scheduled Pub** | |
| | |
| **Fee** | $266 **Fee (Foreign)** |
| **Terms** | on pub |
| **Copies Required** | |
| **Acknowledgement** | |
| | |
| | ☒ Paid **Date** 5/1/1990 ☒ Copies Received |
| **Pub Date** | 6/1/1990 **Pub Time** June 1990 |
| **Pub Title** | The Legend of Slappy Hooper |
| | |
| **Notes** | |
| ☒ PUBLISHED | |
| ☐ CANCELED | |

Story and Article Sales Database

| | | | | | |
|---|---|---|---|---|---|
| **Title** | The Legend of Lightning Larry | | | | |
| **Work #** | 008 | **Type** picture book | **Sub #** 433 | **Book Sale #** 2 | |

| | |
|---|---|
| **Contract Date** | 4/8/1991     **Negotiator** AS |
| **Publisher** | Scribners, Atheneum     **Parent** Macmillan, S&S |
| **Acquirer** | Clare Costello |
| **Market Type** | book     **Market Age** ○ Adult ● Kid |

| | |
|---|---|
| **Rights Type** | ● Primary ○ Sub     **Sub Type** |
| **Territory** |     **Language**     **Term** |
| **Rights Retained** | right to publish in a reader's theater anthology |

| | |
|---|---|
| **Advance** | $5000     **Payment** on signing |
| **Royalty Base** | ● List ○ Net |
| **Hardcover Royalty** | 5%     **Escalation** none |
| **Softcover Royalty** | 3%     **Escalation** none |
| **Statements Due** | 6/30, 12/30     **Royalties Due** 6/30, 12/30 |
| **Author Copies** | 15     **Author Discount** 50% |

| | |
|---|---|
| **Pub Date** | 3/30/1993     **Pub Time** Spring 1993 |
| **Pub Title** | The Legend of Lightning Larry |

| | |
|---|---|
| **Notes** | |

☒ PUBLISHED
☐ CANCELED

Book Sales Database

As you'd expect, I've also replaced my index-card address files with fully searchable and sortable data on all my professional contacts. In fact, I have eight contact databases, with different sets of fields for different contact types! My publisher and periodical databases, for example, have pop-up lists for an individual's job type—editorial, production, and so on. The periodical database also has room for two mailing addresses— one for manuscripts and general business, another for sending books for review. This lets me easily print out reviewer mailing labels to send to my publishers as my books come out.

| Name | Costello, Clare |
| --- | --- |
| City | New York |

| State | NY | Zip | 10022 | Country | USA |
| --- | --- | --- | --- | --- | --- |

| Address | Clare Costello |
| --- | --- |
| | Scribners Books for Young Readers |
| | 866 Third Ave |
| | New York, NY 10022 |

| Phone1 | 212-702-2000 |
| --- | --- |
| Phone2 | |
| Phone3 | |
| Email | |
| ▼▼▼ | |

| Type | ind | Job | editorial |
| --- | --- | --- | --- |
| Medium | book | Group | Macmillan |
| Category | general | | |

Special Interest ☐ Only

☒ Children's  ☒ Mine  ☐ Review Copy  ☐ Comps

Notes

---

| Name | Riverbank Review |
| --- | --- |
| City | Minneapolis |

| State | MN | Zip | 55403 | Country | USA |
| --- | --- | --- | --- | --- | --- |

| Address | Review Address |
| --- | --- |
| Martha Beck, Editor | Riverbank Review |
| Riverbank Review | Attn: Book Reviews |
| 1624 Harmon Place, #305 | 1624 Harmon Place, #305 |
| Minneapolis, MN 55403 | Minneapolis, MN 55403 |

| Phone1 | 612-486-5690 |
| --- | --- |
| Phone2 | |
| Phone3 | |
| Email | beck@bitstream.net |
| ▼▼▼ | www.riverbankreview.com |

| Type | org | Job | |
| --- | --- | --- | --- |
| Medium | mag, Web | Group | |
| Category | books | | |

Special Interest ☐ Only

☐ Children's  ☐ Mine  ☒ Review Copy  ☐ Comps  ☐ Ads

Notes  met Martha Beck at 2001 ALA, S.F.

Publisher and Periodical Databases

My favorite trick in a contact database is to set up separate fields for name, city, state, zip, and country, but add an extra field for the entire mailing address in one piece. (You can do this only if your program allows line breaks within fields.) This makes for some double typing, but it lets me just as easily copy or print an address as sort on it. It also lets me put last name first in the name field, making it possible to sort by an individual's name, while I can still print it in normal order on envelopes and labels.

Maintaining a set of databases takes a significant commitment of time and effort. Like the computer in general, it doesn't save you work, but it does help you organize your work more efficiently and accomplish more. So, if you're overwhelmed by a mass of index cards, or tired of searching for crucial bits of paper, databases may be just what you need.

# Business Forms for the Children's Writer

Writers have various way to keep records—charts, index cards, or as I've described before, databases. But sometimes you need not only to keep records but also to send out that information to others—perhaps in a contract for signing, or in an invoice for payment. For that, you're best served by business forms. And once you have them, you'll likely find extra uses for them too.

As one example, let me share a form that has proven especially useful to me: my Author Appearances form—or as my musical past has inspired me to call it, my "gig sheet." It's used for school visits, bookstore signings, conference appearances, and any other event where I have to present myself. Space is included on the form for each important detail of both the event and my presentation.

A database expert might prefer to set this up as a report to be generated by a database app. Personally, I'm more comfortable with word processors, so I've constructed it as a single-page document in Microsoft Word. The heart of the form is a two-column table with invisible borders. The content labels are placed in the left column, and my data goes on the right.

Though the form is nominally designed as an invoice, it's much more versatile than that. In fact, for any particular gig, it's likely to be used first as a scratchpad. People who want to engage me will usually call to make the initial arrangements. When they do, I grab a blank gig sheet from a stack at my desk and jot down notes. Before ending the call, I can quickly look over the sheet to make sure nothing vital is missing.

Date Paid _____

## Author Appearance Invoice—Aaron Shepard

Presentation date:

Organizer:

Address:


Phone:

Contact:

Contact address:


Contact phone:

Contact fax:

Contact email:

Event:

Event time:

Presentation:

Presentation time:

Location:


Length:

Payment:

Payment Due:

Miscellaneous:




Signature: _____

P.O. Box 555 • Hometown, WA 55555 USA • 555-555-5555 • AS@aaronshep.com

**Gig Sheet**

# Author Appearance Invoice—Aaron Shepard

| Presentation date: | ¤ | ¤ |
|---|---|---|
| Organizer: | ¤ | ¤ |
| Address: | ¤ | ¤ |
| Phone: | ¤ | ¤ |
| Contact: | ¤ | ¤ |
| Contact address: | ¤ | ¤ |
| Contact phone: | ¤ | ¤ |
| Contact fax: | ¤ | ¤ |
| Contact email: | ¤ | ¤ |
| Event: | ¤ | ¤ |
| Event time: | ¤ | ¤ |
| Presentation: | ¤ | ¤ |
| Presentation time: | ¤ | ¤ |
| Location: | ¤ | ¤ |
| Length: | ¤ | ¤ |
| Payment: | ¤ | ¤ |
| Payment Due: | ¤ | ¤ |
| Miscellaneous: | ¤ | ¤ |

Signature: _____

**Gig Sheet in Draft View**

The next step—or the first one, if arrangements have been made by email—is to make a more legible copy, again by hand. This is the copy I use in preparing for the gig. When not on my desk, this copy stays in my filing cabinet in a folder labeled "Gigs—To Come," filed there in order of gig date. Each week, I check the folder to see what's coming up. And of course, when I make the appearance, I carry the gig sheet along for easy reference.

After the gig, the form goes back into my filing cabinet in one of two folders. If I appeared without charge, or if I received payment during the event (as I try to do), the sheet goes into "Gigs—Paid." Otherwise, it goes into "Gigs—Unpaid," and I keep an eye on it to make sure it doesn't stay there too long.

At the beginning of each school year, I start a new "Gigs—Paid" folder and mark the old one with the school year just past. The gig sheets in this old folder then become part of a permanent record. This is especially helpful if I'm ever hired for a repeat appearance. Among other things, I can tell whether I need to modify my presentation to keep from repeating myself.

If I actually have to send the form as an invoice, I fill it in once more, but this time on my computer. I insert only the information needed, then print and sign it. I keep a special multi-page document for this, adding new copies of the form as needed, separated by page breaks. After printing the individual invoice, I leave it in the document in case I later have to change or add to it and reprint.

Note that I could use this form as a contract as well as an invoice, simply by adding a signature line for the organizer plus date lines for both of us. In fact, that's how this form started out. But I found I didn't need contracts for author appearances, as long as I required the organizer to purchase my ticket and arrange my accommodation.

Another form I've used often is for rights sales. A form like this is handy if subsidiary rights are not all handled for you by a publisher or agent. It can act as an invoice, a formal notice of permission, or both. Like the gig sheet, it can also be used for recordkeeping and payment tracking, but I do that now with a database instead. In fact, when I need the form filled out, I mostly drag and drop the entries from my database.

Nowadays, I'll do almost anything to avoid dealing with my own book sales—even for books I've self published. But if you find yourself selling directly to bookstores or event organizers, you could probably benefit from a book sales invoice too.

Though a business form may take a while to set up and perfect, it can save you time in the long run and help you stay organized. You can't ask more of it than that!

Date Paid _____

# Rights Invoice and Authorization—Aaron Shepard

Date:

Buyer:

Contact:

Address:


Phone:

Fax:

Email:

Title of Work:

Rights granted:

Purchased for:


Appearance date:

Fee:

Payment Due:

Copies required:

Acknowledgement:



Miscellaneous:




Signature: _____

P.O. Box 555 • Hometown, WA 55555 USA • 555-555-5555 • AS@aaronshep.com

## Rights Sheet

# Aaron Shepard

P. O. Box 555        Hometown, Washington 55555 USA        555-555-5555

## Invoice

Invoice date:

Sold to:

Your order no.:

Terms:

Shipped to:

Shipping date:

Shipped via:

| Ord'd | Ship'd | Title | List | Disc. | Net |
|-------|--------|-------|------|-------|-----|
|       |        |       |      |       |     |
|       |        |       |      |       |     |
|       |        |       |      |       |     |
|       |        |       |      |       |     |
|       |        |       |      |       |     |

| | |
|---|---|
| Subtotal | |
| Tax | |
| Shipping | |
| **Total** | |
| Received | |
| **Balance due** | |

Please pay from this invoice if due.
No statement will be sent.

Refer to this invoice by date.

*Thank you!*

AS@aaronshep.com • www.aaronshep.com

**Book Sales Invoice**

# The Magic of Reading to Children

Authors have many opportunities to read their stories, and children love to hear them. If you can bring your stories to life, you unlock their potential for young listeners—and perhaps the potential of reading in general. You are living proof that reading is not boring!

With some help from our friends in storytelling and reader's theater, here are some hints for effective reading.

• If you can, check out the room and P.A. system ahead of time to take care of potential problems. (Just to be safe, I usually bring along my $100 karaoke machine, which is better than many school P.A. systems.)

• For a forceful presence, stand up. For a more relaxed image, use a stool or chair. But in all cases make sure you're high enough for everyone to see your face.

• Introduce the book by showing its cover and announcing the title, to help your listeners find it later. Your introduction can also mention something intriguing about the story, or some background on how it was written, or on what it means to you. But if your listeners don't already know the plot, don't give it away!

• Wait for silence before reading. After that, DO NOT stop at every little noise. If the story is working, noise will be minimal and will probably taper off, because your audience will be listening intently. If someone is making a disturbance you can't ignore, you can perhaps tactfully ask him or her to stop, explaining that it distracts you. But DON'T COME DOWN HARD!

Remember, you're a celebrity to those kids, and an attack by you could be devastating, with long-term effect.

• If you choose to show the pictures while reading, hold the book to the side at about eye-level, grasping the bottom edge with one hand and looking sideways to read. Turn the pages by reaching up without moving the book. Remember to swing the book toward the sides of your audience once or twice for each illustration.

If you're *not* showing pictures, hold the book in front with one hand, leaving the other hand free for gesturing and page turning. With a hardcover, the spine can lie loose in your palm, or you can grasp the top edge. Keep the book low enough so you can see everyone up to the front row. Remember, if you can't see them, they can't see you!

• Give your listeners the full force of you. When sitting or standing still, keep your back straight and face your listeners squarely. Don't sit or stand sideways, slump, sag, or shift from foot to foot.

• Make sure you are heard well. If using a mike on a stand, keep the mike at a steady distance—close enough so it picks you up properly, but not so close it distorts. If *not* using a mike, speak loudly, aiming your voice at the back row.

Good volume requires good breath support, so be sure you breathe from your diaphragm. This is the muscle that lies below your chest and controls the expansion of your lower lungs. To check yourself, place your hand lightly on your stomach and inhale deeply. If you're using your diaphragm properly, it will push your stomach *out*. (The extra air in your lungs may make you a bit dizzy till you get used to it.)

• Make your words ring, by pronouncing each syllable distinctly. (Tongue twisters provide good practice.)

• Take your time and read slowly. Your listeners must re-create the scenes in their imaginations, and that takes time and unhurried concentration. Many readers will speed up when they sense they're losing their listeners' attention. In most cases, they should instead slow down.

• Look out at your listeners as much as you can—ideally about half the time, and especially at the ends of sentences. To do this, know your selection well enough so you can look at the page and "gather" the words ahead of where you're speaking. With a book held in front, you can keep your place in the text with a finger or thumb, running it down the page or along the edge.

When reading a page in front of you, lower only your eyes, not your whole head. If you are also looking up often, you will hardly seem to be reading at all, and the effect will be akin to true storytelling.

• Use variety to put life into the story. Vary each of the following: pitch, volume, tone, speed, and rhythm.

• Respect and use pauses—between clauses, sentences, paragraphs, and scenes. Today's editors may delight in throwing out commas, but you need to read them back in!

• Don't be afraid to gesture and move around. Movement adds interest and holds attention. And a little miming is fun as well.

• Don't forget sound effects, either!

• Make the characters live. Try to sound and look and move as you think each character would. Express how the character feels by your voice, face, and gesture. If possible, make each character sound different from other characters and from the narrator.

When using special character voices for dialog, make sure you drop those voices for the "tag lines"—the "he said" and "she said" phrases. These should be in your normal narrator voice. However, if you're using special voices, most of the tag lines can just be left out.

• If you're adventurous, try using different "focuses." Most of the time when you're not looking at your book, you'll be looking straight at your listeners ("audience focus"). But when portraying a character, you might pretend to be looking at someone or something over your listeners' heads ("offstage focus"). Remember to switch back to audience focus for tag lines you retain.

If you're reading a scene with two characters conversing, you can try "cross focus"—turning to a different 45 degree angle for each character. If the characters are supposed to be at different heights, you can also look upward and downward.

• Make your ending definite by reading the last words slowly and with rhythm. Everyone recognizes the ending "*happily ever after.*" But the same effect can be achieved with almost any words by reading them in a "slow three." (As an author, you can make sure your stories end with appropriate rhythm.)

• When you've finished, pause a moment for your listeners to return from the world you and they have created. Then close the book, again show the cover, and repeat the title.

Good reading requires practice. A tape recorder and a full-length mirror can give you valuable feedback. Also helpful is listening to professional storytellers and readers, live or on tape. But don't take it all *too* seriously. Even without trying, you'll get better as you go. Besides, you're a professional *author,* not a professional *performer*—so no one will expect you to be perfect.

Relax, play, enjoy yourself. If there's nothing else you give your listeners, you can show them reading is fun!

# Tinker, Tailor, Writer, Storyteller

Writing, they say, is a lonely profession. But there are ways to ease that. You can join a critique group. You can go to conferences. You can become a storyteller.

I have found storytelling to be a wonderful way to get away from the computer and come face to face with charmed and charming children, so eager to hear the stories I offer. I may feel like the lowest of the low when rejection slips crowd my mailbox, but in front of the kids I am King.

Besides the psychic boost, telling traditional folktales has helped develop my picture book writing. This is largely because of what those tales leave out. Setting is seldom more than mentioned, while characterization is limited to broad strokes. Internal musings are nearly forbidden. Flashbacks don't happen. Abstractions are taboo.

With the trappings removed, what's left is elemental Story—action, dialog, and word play, relentlessly impelling the story on a direct path from beginning to end. This, of course, is the aim of the picture book writer. And I can't help but get a feel for it when I learn and tell folktales.

Storytelling helps my writing even more directly by letting me test my own stories in performance. We authors are often warned that the kids we know don't make good judges. But, let me tell you, a roomful of young strangers makes a *very* good judge. It lets me know each moment if the story is working. Then I can take the story back to the computer and strengthen

From the *SCBW Bulletin,* March–April 1992.

it before the next trial-by-fire. The result is a 100% kid-tested story.

I also find that practicing and performing a story-in-progress helps me come up with the simplest and most natural wording for what I want to say. The story becomes more readable, and a better candidate for bedtime and story hours.

In one case, I combined storytelling and writing in an even more integral way. This was when I retold the folktale, "The Boy Who Went Forth to Learn What Fear Was"—or, as I renamed it, "The Boy Who Wanted the Willies." The story is set mainly in a haunted castle, where a string of scary visitors fails to make the least impression on a ridiculously fearless hero.

The problem I saw with the tale was that many of the original incidents wouldn't click with today's kids. I had to find ones that would.

So I began performing the story as an improvisation piece. I got the boy into the castle in the dead of night, the clock struck one, and "something very scary happened. What was it?" One of the kids would tell me, and then I would invent on the spot how the hero dealt with it. The clock would then strike two, and so on, until I was ready to wind up the story.

In this way, I got a list of about fifteen scary incidents that would work with today's kids. When I was ready to put the story on disk, I just picked the best incidents and stretched them a bit. (But I still perform the story as an improv. It's more fun!)

Storytelling also helps me in promoting myself as a children's writer. By going public, I'm creating an ever-larger audience for my children's books, as well as opportunities for direct book sales. And my acquired skill in captivating crowds of squirrelly youngsters makes me a natural for author visits, writer workshops, and other such events.

One warning: Storytelling requires a large investment of time for finding and learning stories. As you get more serious, performances and marketing can also take big chunks. A writer with limited time might do better sticking to the keyboard.

But I'm not sure I could ever give it up. It's too much fun. And I wouldn't be the same writer without it.

# Works in Progress

The Internet has brought remarkable opportunities not only in education and literature but also in the interface between them. Watching the Internet's early growth, I began to dream of sending my unfinished stories to some of the children I wrote for, to garner comments that would help me in revision. By 1995, the technology for such a project was at hand.

In early January of that year, I composed an invitation entitled "Works in Progress: An Online Experiment." This invitation was sent to various discussion lists and newsgroups for teachers and librarians, as well as to teachers identified from the member directory of America Online. (I learned only later that AOL prohibited that!)

My posts and emails brought the invitation directly to the attention of thousands, and from there it was shared—online and off—with many more. Here in part is what it said:

> If you are working with young people in grades 3–6 in the first quarter of 1995, I invite you to take part in a collaborative online experiment in literature and education.
>
> Works in Progress is a program in which educators and librarians will receive stories as email from an established children's author. These "works in progress" have not yet reached final form. Participants will be asked to share the stories with young people and to relay

---

Updated from the *SCBWI Bulletin*, August–September 1996.

comments back to the author, as well as to comment themselves.

While the author gains valuable feedback, kids will gain interest in and appreciation of the creative process—and both kids and adults will enjoy the opportunity to influence stories headed for publication.

The stories selected are "The Man Who Knew Everything: A Tale of Iran," and "Nonviolence: A Buddhist Fable." Participants may respond to one or both of the stories. Supplementary materials include a letter to the kids, suggested questions for discussion, and an author profile.

There is no charge for the program. To receive the materials, just send me an email request at one of the addresses below. Stories will be sent to the return address at the head of your email message.

The response was overwhelming. Within a few weeks, I had received requests from 500 email addresses around the world. Many of these addresses represented multiple classrooms, or even multiple schools. As it turned out, most of the signups failed to return comments—primarily due to time constraints, judging from explanations I received. Still, by around the deadline of March 1, comments had been emailed from about 200 addresses. By my best estimate, about 5,000 students took part!

Luckily, I had the foresight to request that the responses be collective, rather than from individual students. Even so, the comments amassed into a two-inch pile of printouts. My job then was to sift through the pile, determine the predominant reactions, and use them to guide my revision of both stories.

This job was complete by mid-April. At that time, I sent my revisions to all participants. With the revisions went a report on the most important comments I had received, what I had used, what I had decided against using, and my reasons. And I cautioned everyone that the stories were still not in final form—because I keep revising and improving my stories right up to publication, and sometimes after! I also described my plans for getting each story published, and promised to send major news of my progress.

Was the project successful? Wildly so. For my own part, I gained valuable insights into how kids were able to deal with these two stories in particular and multicultural literature in general. Both stories became stronger, and I gained a better idea of each one's potential.

Perhaps as a result, I was able to report sales of both stories by November. "Nonviolence," now retitled "How Violence Is Ended," eventually appeared in *Cricket*, Australia's *School Magazine*, and *Parabola*. "The Man Who Knew Everything" too appeared in *School Magazine* and *Parabola*; and retitled as "Forty Fortunes," it went on to become a picture book from Clarion.

Aside from that, the project introduced me as an author to thousands of enthusiastic teachers, librarians, and students I might otherwise never have reached. Numerous schools inquired about visits, and one school flew me to Indiana. Another high point came when two teachers organized an online chat with me for thirty classes all across the continent, meeting in the Electronic Schoolhouse of America Online—years before virtual author visits became common.

As for benefits to the participants, here are some of the teachers' own words:

> "I can't tell you how inspired my students have found your efforts to make your stories better and better by

rewriting and revising. They are so much more enthusiastic about revising their own stories."

"It has been one of the best things we have been able to do with them this year. One of the most telling things was when they realized you actually had a reason for changes you made and didn't make."

"The whole idea was wonderful. It lets them see the purpose to the writing process when they can see it put to use in the 'real world' of literature!"

"This was a terrific experience for them. Not only did it help them develop critical thinking, it made them feel VERY important helping a real author."

"For many students, this was among the first activities that excited them about literature. They could make a difference; language was real and with a purpose."

As valuable as the project was, I never did find time to repeat it. But this and similar opportunities await other authors willing to use the Internet to bridge the gap between themselves and their readers—not only in promoting published work but in sharing the heady process of creation.

# Saving *The Sea King's Daughter*

I should have been suspicious the first time.

Like most other moderately successful children's authors, I've had my share of books going out of print. My response over the years has been to immediately request a reversion of rights, and to encourage the book's illustrator to do the same. My idea was, with emerging technologies, I might one day be able to reissue the books myself.

So, when my picture book *The Sea King's Daughter* went out of print in both hardcover and paperback, I had my agent send the reversion request. But this time was different. After a month or two, I was informed that, instead of reverting the rights, Simon & Schuster was restoring the book to print.

I took that as a pleasant surprise. It had never happened before, but *The Sea King's Daughter* was one of my biggest sellers and my most honored book—illustrated as it was by the world-class artist Gennady Spirin—so it didn't seem unreasonable. But a year or so later, the same thing happened with my *next* S&S book to go out of print. And this was one of my *worst* sellers—a highly unlikely candidate for reprinting.

This time, I *did* get suspicious. So, I ordered copies of both books from Amazon. Sure enough, they were both print-on-demand books from the biggest of the POD services, Lightning Source.

OK, you may be wondering how I knew that, so let me back up a bit. Since 1999, alongside my career as a children's author, I've been building a profitable career as a self publisher of adult

---

From the *SCBWI Bulletin,* September–October 2011.

nonfiction using POD, and particularly Lightning Source. In fact, I've written and published several popular books helping others do the same. So, when I saw those two picture book reprints, the last pages told me at once they were Lightning Source books. (In general, if the last page shows nothing but a bar code and text at the bottom, you're looking at POD.)

I should also explain I have nothing at all against publishers putting their books into POD, even if it means keeping the rights forever. In fact, I welcome it. Keeping my books permanently in print is exactly what I want them to do! There was just one problem.

*The Sea King's Daughter* looked terrible. I don't mean just a little off, as paperback reprints tend to look, but really, truly terrible. The colors were much too light and much too green. A book that had been honored by *The New York Times* as one of the best-illustrated of the year had been reduced to a sickly, horrid embarrassment.

So, I did what any overconfident children's author with a meager background in POD book design would do. I offered to create new production files for Simon & Schuster.

They actually accepted that offer. But after I realized just how much work it would be, I decided to up the ante and try to publish it myself. S&S generously offered to revert my rights for that, but I had never been able to connect with Gennady Spirin directly, and I wasn't sure I could make the necessary arrangements with him. So instead, I *bought* the reprint rights from S&S for both text and illustrations. (And yes, I later received my author percentage of the rights fee.)

Now, if you think this is an article encouraging you to go out and reprint your old picture books, guess again. I had no idea what I was getting into, and the farther in I went, the worse it got. Here's a brief litany of what I encountered, along with my solutions. (For a more detailed discussion, see the longer version of this article on my Publishing Page at www.newselfpublishing.com.)

**Problem:** S&S no longer had either digital files or original art for the book, so I planned to scan and descreen the old page proofs I'd saved all these years. Halfway through the scanning, though, I realized the proofs were not in good enough shape for the job.

**Solution:** Order a new set of proofs from the printer for a breathtaking sum of money.

**Problem:** The new proofs were sent not as spreads but as signatures—huge sheets of paper with eight pages per side, and with most double-page illustrations separated into two non-adjoining pieces.

**Solution:** Cut out the individual pages carefully and count on a glued binding to hide imperfections at the gutter.

**Problem:** Halfway through the scanning and descreening of the *new* proofs, my trusty old large-format scanner began to break down, with no repair parts available.

**Solution:** Buy a new large-format scanner for a sum greater than all my expenses so far. Also, buy an expensive third-party scanning program to make the scanner work properly with my Mac, then spend a couple of weeks learning how to use the new program. (It's a good thing this project was for love, not money!)

**Problem:** Because of a satin finish on the new proofs for cover and jacket, they were already curled and marred beyond usefulness for scanning.

**Solution:** Entirely redesign the cover around an inside illustration.

**Problem:** The original title page was designed with title words stretching across the gutter. That was fine on the flat pages of a sewn hardcover, but not on the curved pages of a glued paperback.

**Solution:** Entirely redesign the title page.

**Problem:** The original typeface for the book was mostly too delicate for the low resolution of today's color POD. I knew it would look even worse if scanned along with the illustrations and screened by the printer. But for most pages, that seemed inevitable, because type was placed *over* painted backgrounds.

**Solution:** Typeset the entire book from scratch, using the lovely original typeface for display type but replacing it with something sturdier for body type. I managed to remove *all* old type from my scans without noticeably harming backgrounds by use of "Content-Aware Fill," a brand-new feature of Adobe Photoshop CS5. When an area with type was deleted, Photoshop filled in with the pattern of surrounding areas! I could then place new type over the same spot.

**Problem:** For color printing, Lightning Source imposes a number of odd and restrictive requirements. For a glued binding, each page must include at least a narrow white margin at the gutter, even if that fell in the middle of a two-page illustration. Pictures that bleed off the page must do it by a full quarter inch—more bleed than was available on my proofs. Also, none of the trim sizes offered by Lightning matched the dimension ratio of the original book.

**Solution:** Switch to CreateSpace—Amazon's POD operation—which did not impose such requirements and had just begun offering custom trim sizes. (This switch, though, came at the expense of Lightning's much superior distribution).

**Problem:** At first, I'd intended to match as closely as possible the color from my proofs and my hardcover copies. But the more I studied those and played with my scans, the more I became aware of problems with contrast and color cast in the original edition, despite the acclaim the book had received.

**Solution:** Use Photoshop to adjust the contrast and remove the color cast, bringing out colors in the illustrations more brilliant than I had ever known were there.

**Problem:** CreateSpace, like Lightning, declines to provide a color profile for its POD presses and paper, making it impossible to target an appropriate print color space.

**Solution:** For Lightning, I had already found a more appropriate color profile on the Web and had also worked out a color conversion process to apply less ink to the paper if needed. Though I could probably have used the same solution for this book at CreateSpace, a tech there confided that I could just supply my files in the common Adobe RGB color space with profile embedded, and the color would be converted automatically and correctly.

It worked! The colors were lovely. The printing was not as sharp and clean as it would have been on better paper, but overall, the book was well within the expected quality range of a reprint—and *many* times better than the disaster from S&S.

And so, *The Sea King's Daughter* is back, in a brand new paperback 15th Anniversary Edition from my own Skyhook Press. Was it worth it?

Probably not. If I had it to do over, I doubt I would. On the other hand, now that I've done it . . .

OK, I admit it. I'm raring to reprint more of my books. And after that, maybe some originals? I do have all those unsold manuscripts. . . .

# From Picture Book to Ebook

You've heard of trying to fit a square peg in a round hole. But what about a landscape JPEG on a portrait page?

Welcome to the wonderful world of ebooks.

In the migration from print to ebook, illustrated books like children's picture books present a special challenge. It's relatively simple to pour the straight text of a novel into an ebook container. But with a picture book, what do you do with pictures of various shapes and sizes, all carefully laid out in relation to specific text, when you have no idea what size or shape of screen it will be displayed on?

Since the rise of the Kindle and of its competitor ebook format EPUB, the dominant ebook layout has been *flowing text*. In this layout, text is automatically resized, repositioned, and repaged as needed to fit screens of any size and shape. It's similar to what you get in a word processor, and that's normally what you'd use to compose it.

But to handle cases like picture books, both Kindle and EPUB enable books to be produced instead in *fixed format*. This places text and pictures in exact positions, like you'd get from a page layout app. Most picture ebooks are now produced this way.

There are good reasons why fixed format has become so popular for children's picture books. The main one is that it allows older books to be converted to ebooks without being completely redesigned! And in turn, that has made it possible for ebook providers like Amazon, Apple, and Barnes & Noble to perform many of the early conversions for major publishers at no charge—just to quickly get a large number of picture books on sale.

Still, fixed format has never been a perfect solution for such conversions, or even a very good one. Many if not most picture books are laid out with double-page spreads—so fixed format for these books means fitting two book pages onto a single screen in landscape mode.

If the individual pages aren't too large or too wide, that *can* work on a large tablet like the full-size iPad. But what about the smaller screen on the iPad mini, or on most of the Kindle Fires? Or nowadays, even on a smart phone? On such devices, the text can become too small to be read comfortably, while pictures can become too small to have much impact.

To compensate for tiny text and pictures in fixed format, the producers use tricks like letting the reader click on text or pictures to enlarge them. But seriously, is that the reader's job? Shouldn't these elements be sized effectively to start with?

What's more, fixed-format ebooks often can't be read on ebook readers with e-ink screens. Many of those readers aren't advanced enough to display fixed format, while on others, landscape mode may be a hassle or not even an option.

The truth is, fixed format is a lazy workaround to the problem of picture ebooks. Whether a picture book is converted from print or published first as an ebook, it should be designed or redesigned specially for the variety of devices it will be read on. And that means designing as flowing text.

Flowing text, though, presents its own challenges, especially when it comes to illustrations. So far, I've tackled these with two picture books of mine converted from print, *The Baker's Dozen* and *The Legend of Lightning Larry*, both originally from Atheneum; *The Adventures of Mouse Deer*, with stories of mine that first appeared in Australia's *School Magazine*; and *Christmas Truce*, a picture book I self published from scratch.

The main challenge is to make sure the illustrations are as large as possible. Ideally, you want them to fill the screen—which, after all, may be small to begin with. Because of differently shaped screens, though, you can't avoid sometimes getting extra space either at the sides or at top and bottom, depending on the device. That means that sometimes there will be space for words on the same page, and sometimes not.

So, to keep my layouts consistent while also accommodating large picture sizes, I like to completely separate text and pictures, starting a new page for each. At the same time, I generally try to make each illustration come right after text that relates to it. Sometimes that means taking text from a single page of the printed book and splitting it, placing some of the text on the page before the picture and some on the page after.

Text pages without illustration can visually bore a child who's being read to. So, to make up for the absence, I usually add small pictures as ornaments at the heads of those pages. Sometimes, the illustrator has obligingly placed suitable ornaments in the printed book; other times, they can be extracted from the illustrations. In *The Legend of Lightning Larry*, for example, many illustrations include a number of small lightning bolts. It was simple enough to isolate and combine them, forming several patterns I could insert on my text pages in a repeating cycle.

Unfortunately, just placing an illustration on its own page doesn't mean it will fill much of that page, because there's a catch. Most picture book illustrations are in landscape mode—wider than tall. Ebook devices, though, are mostly read in portrait mode—taller than wide. For a picture to display at a good size, it must roughly match the screen shape. But how can you adapt a landscape picture to a portrait screen?

If you're starting from scratch, you can make sure the illustrations are created in portrait mode to begin with—as I did with *Christmas Truce*. That's always best. But what about illustrations designed for print? The picture on a double-page spread may have a width that is several times the height.

I've found there's no single solution to the problem of landscape pictures, and there might even be times you can't do a thing. But so far, I've been able to handle every situation with one of three strategies. Here they are, with sample illustrations of my own from my upcoming picture book *Why the Author Should Have Stuck to Writing*.

**1. Crop the picture.** You can sometimes improve the orientation of the illustration simply by removing parts of it. This would work, for instance, if your main subject is near the center, with less important matter to the right and left. Take this picture of my hero, Bobby Bitmap, with a row of trees behind him.

Before Cropping

As much as the trees add to the picture, you *could* do without most of them. If I crop away the outer ones, the vital part of the picture will appear much larger, while you still see enough trees to get the idea.

After Cropping

*Adventures in Writing for Children*

**2. Divide the picture.** Though you would obviously prefer to keep an illustration all on one page, sometimes it makes better sense to split it between two. You might do that, for instance, if the main subjects of the picture are divided cleanly between the left and right sides.

Here's Bobby again, along with my heroine, Vicky Vector. (That's Vicky on the left and Bobby on the right. Or vice versa. I forget.) First let's see them together.

Before Dividing

And now, divided to fall on two pages.

After Dividing, Left Half

After Dividing, Right Half

One thing that can help this to work is if the original illustration shows action and response. The character on the left does something, and the character on the right reacts to it. So, the sequence is logical when you divide the picture, with one part following the next. If the dynamic was reversed—action on right, response on left—the division wouldn't work at all, because the parts would be out of order—at least for a book in English or any other left-to-right language. In such a case, you could try flipping the original picture so it comes out the other way.

Divided pictures can feel overdone if a book has too many, especially if the same characters keep appearing in them. If you find they're bogging you down, you might sometimes just use the more important half of the illustration and drop the other.

**3. Stack the picture.** With an especially wide illustration, you might find it best to divide it into two or three panels and reposition them vertically. Here are Bobby and Vicky waving to each other from different points along a river.

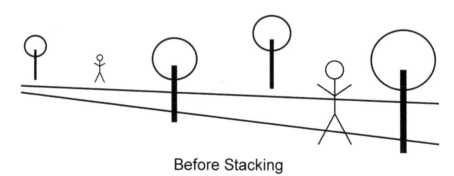

Before Stacking

And now the stacked version.

After Stacking

I've positioned the panels top to bottom corresponding to the original's left to right. Also, I've made sure the "weightiest" panel is at bottom to keep the illustration from feeling top-heavy. Finally, the sequence of panels is made clearer by the perspective, with the continuously enlarged river acting as a thread to visually tie the panels together.

Note that I've recombined these panels as a *single* picture instead of placing them separately, one after the other. This way, I know for sure they'll appear on the same page.

If the illustrator has done something fancy with picture edges, any crop or division might need follow-up work. For example, for my Mouse Deer stories, the illustrator scalloped the edges of all illustrations. So, when I created new edges, I had to apply my Photoshop tools to scallop the new ones as well. At times, though, you might find that the best way to deal with fancy edges is to just trim them off.

Sometimes getting a picture into portrait orientation is enough to make it display at an adequate size—but often it's not. Assuming you have enough pixels to maintain high resolution, consider cropping in farther, from any or all edges. Remember, the more you remove, the larger the remainder will display. Also keep in mind that extra background details do no good if they're too small to make out.

It's never ideal to alter art, and it's certainly not something to do lightly. But when faced with a choice of either altering a picture or else displaying it at a size too small for appreciation, I'll make the change. After all, the purpose of the ebook isn't to replicate or document the print book but to adapt it to a whole new medium.

In the end, my illustrators seem happy with my careful modifications. And judging by my online reviews, my readers definitely are!

# This Is Not a Test

I regret that I no longer permit use of my stories or scripts for educational testing. I'm sorry for any inconvenience.

It wasn't easy to write. I hate to say no to people. And I don't like turning away money. In fact, it wasn't long ago that I was planning a marketing campaign to sell my writing to test publishers.

But I haven't been able to shake the image of some kid sitting and sweating over one of my stories while struggling to come up with answers to please the teacher. Anxiety, competition, ambition, fear—are these the emotions I want associated with my stories?

I remember hearing Jim Trelease talk about how teachers can and do easily turn kids away from reading by turning it into a chore, a source of information for filling in exercise sheets. In one classroom, a teacher told her students about her reading every night before bedtime and asked why they thought she did that. Their answer: for "practice." Her students didn't understand that people could read for the pleasure of it.

I want my stories to be sources of joy—not achievement, not approval, not advancement. And yes, I do want teachers to use them—in fact, that's what I aim for. But please, not to deaden the love of reading. Not to make students cringe at the sight of a printed page. Not to make them see story as a tool of control.

---

From *Once Upon A Time*, Fall 2005.

And so,

I regret that I no longer permit use of my stories or scripts for educational testing. I'm sorry for any inconvenience.

# What's Good for Business . . .

> Though written during a very different time, this article still holds interest for the light it casts on conditions today.—Aaron

All around us, we hear heralded the phenomenal growth of the children's book industry and the wonderful opportunities this affords. But this incredible growth may ultimately work *against* children's book writers—and children's books themselves.

Let's look at an analogy with the field of urban development. It used to be an unchallenged assumption that cities should grow. Attracting industry meant that jobs would be created, decreasing unemployment. And, as population increased, the tax base would expand, so more services could be provided.

This turned out to be false reasoning. New industry created jobs, but more people came to take those jobs. And increased population expanded the tax base, but the extra taxes collected went for services to the new residents. Meanwhile, quality of life degenerated.

In a similar way, the growth of the children's book industry creates more opportunities for writers. But, as word of those opportunities spread, more writers arrive to take advantage of them. In the end, there may be a greater glut of children's writers than ever.

---

From the *SCBWI Bulletin,* August–September 1996.

But there is an even greater danger from this rapid growth: the commercialization of children's books.

Let's look at another analogy, this time with the field of rock music. In the 1960s, there was a movement of creative rock known as "underground," largely associated with the San Francisco music scene. Nearly commercial-free "underground" FM radio stations sprang up around the country. This movement brought rock music to an unparalleled level of artistic expression.

The problem came when the music grew too popular. When it became obvious that this music could make lots of money, it was bought up. And, when it was bought up, it in effect disappeared.

When big money moves in, creativity, originality, and freedom move out. The reason is risk. When a lot of money is at stake, the investors insist on a safe product. And they get what they want. Formulas reign. Products are geared to the mass market—meaning, the lowest common denominator.

As rock musician David Crosby pointed out, "The only thing you can be consistently is mediocre."

We have already seen this process in the adult book industry. The only likely way to make a living in adult fiction today is genre writing—science fiction, romance, Westerns, and such. A serious novelist finds it harder than ever to be published.

Now let's turn to children's book publishing. Here we find great growth, but much of it in series and "packaged" books. And we writers are subtly and not so subtly encouraged to write "down"—to make our writing accessible to the widest range of reading skills and the most common sensibilities. It seems the more literate and sophisticated children must fend for themselves. They can always turn to the classics.

Really, children's books more and more resemble network TV. Of course, there is still quality programming—"specials"—

but it is gradually being overwhelmed in the marketplace and in the child's mind by series schlock and other types of formula production. For those who like schlock, that's fine. But other kids will wind up with schlock simply because that's what's most available. And the youngest kids can't tell the difference until it's too late.

Compare TV news with the new breed of children's nonfiction book. We are now advised that all such books should be brief and profusely illustrated. These are the same restrictions that force TV news to be shallow. The fact is, some of the most important things we can tell children are hard or impossible to illustrate. We seem to be deciding that these things *will not be said* through nonfiction.

Bigger is not always better. With the growth of the industry, it falls to the real lovers of children's books to slow the gradual slide of the industry into the practices of commercial culture. We can only do this by staying focused on quality. There will always be others to worry about quantity.

# Real Books

I was roaming the exhibit hall at the International Reading Association convention in Anaheim, California. Almost every major children's book publisher was exhibiting. Surrounded by glitz and glamour, I scanned the pretty covers of nice stories in attractive packages—hundreds and hundreds of them.

Then I came to a book that stopped me. It was Mordecai Gerstein's *The Shadow of a Flying Bird*. I had not read the book, but I knew the author's work, and I had read reviews. I knew it was a Jewish fable about death, which the author had retold when his own father died.

It was what I call a *real book*—a book written from the heart and speaking to the heart. And the sight of such a book was like meeting a long-lost friend in the midst of a wasteland. There in the IRA exhibit hall, I cried.

I don't mean to say that Gerstein's book was the only "real book" in the hall. I know there were others. But as Theodore Sturgeon once said, 90% of anything is crap.

Crap is what you get when your goal in publishing is only to turn a profit, or fill a list, or spread a message; or when your goal in writing is only to sell a manuscript, or advance your career, or fill a need.

A real book is what you get when you write or publish because a story fills your heart till it overflows, or tickles your mind till it pops, or burns in your gut till it eats its way out, or lights up your soul till it shines forth.

---

From *Once Upon A Time*, Winter 1996.

If your own story doesn't make you laugh or cry or shiver or ponder or dance—what is it worth?

Real books enrich. Crap merely impresses. Real books dive deep. Crap skims the surface. Real books nourish. Crap is like white bread—mere empty calories.

Our children are fed a steady diet of crap—by TV, by radio, by movies, by books. Seldom does one heart speak to another. Is it any wonder so many of our young people are growing up heartless?

Our children don't need more crap. They need books that help them grow into full human beings. They need books that show them the depths of another person's heart. They need books that change their lives from the inside.

They need real books.

# Kidwriting Quotes

"The best way to have a good idea is to have lots of ideas."

—Linus Pauling

"The function of the overwhelming majority of your artwork is simply to teach you how to make the small fraction of your artwork that soars."

—David Bayles and Ted Orland, *Art and Fear*

"Obscurity is a far greater threat to authors than piracy."

—Tim O'Reilly

"The time has come for writers to become inaccessible again. The reason is not some kind of 'mystique' that makes people curious (though it helps), but the fact that no real writers ever lay down anything real in public—they work in solitude, they think hard, and their thoughts are rarely nice or 'friendly.'"

—Andrei Codrescu, *Publishers Weekly*,
Jan. 31, 2011

"When critics say a writer is beginning to come into his own, they mean he has finally discovered the single theme which bulks largest in his intellect, his imagination, and his emotions."

—Robi Macauley and George Lanning,
*Technique in Fiction*

"Writing a book is an adventure. To begin with, it is a toy and an amusement; then it becomes a mistress, and then it becomes a master, and then a tyrant. The last phase is that, just as you are about to be reconciled to your servitude, you kill the monster and fling him out to the public."

—Winston Churchill

"Words are like harpoons. Once they go in, they are very hard to pull out."

—Fred Hoyle

"You have to write whichever book it is that wants to be written. And then, if it's going to be too difficult for grownups, you write it for children."

—Madeleine L'Engle

"I'm not writing to make anyone's children feel safe."

—J. K. Rowling

"It is as easy to dream up a book as it is hard to write one."

—Balzac

"Quantity produces quality. If you write only a few things, you're doomed."

—Ray Bradbury

"It does not seem to me that I have the right to foist a story on people, most of whom are children who should be learning all the time, unless I am learning from it too."

—Diana Wynne Jones

"You have to understand, my dears, that the shortest distance between truth and a human being is a story."

—Anthony de Mello, *One Minute Wisdom*

"Writing, for me, is a little like wood carving. You find the lump of tree (the big central theme that gets you started), and you start cutting the shape that you think you want it to be. But you find, if you do it right, that the wood has a grain of its own (characters develop and present new insights, concentrated thinking about the story opens new avenues). If you're sensible, you work with the grain and, if you come across a knot hole, you incorporate that into the design. This is not the same as 'making it up as you go along'; it's a very careful process of control."

—Terry Pratchett, in back matter for
*A Hat Full of Sky*

"I don't want to write for adults. I want to write for readers who can perform miracles. Only children perform miracles when they read."

—Astrid Lindgren

"There have been great societies that did not use the wheel, but there have been no societies that did not tell stories."

—Ursula K. LeGuin

"The tale is often wiser than the teller."

—Susan Fletcher, *Shadow Spinner*

"In our time, when the literature for adults is deteriorating, good books for children are the only hope, the only refuge."

—Isaac Bashevis Singer

"'Thou shalt not' is soon forgotten, but 'Once upon a time' lasts forever."

—Philip Pullman, 1996 Carnegie Medal acceptance speech

"If stories come to you, care for them. And learn to give them away where they are needed. Sometimes a person needs a story more than food to stay alive."

—Barry Lopez, *Crow and Weasel*

"If a book comes from the heart, it will contrive to reach other hearts."

—Thomas Carlyle

"Story is the vehicle we use to make sense of our lives in a world that often defies logic."

—Jim Trelease

"Of course it's true, but it may not have happened."

—Patricia Polacco's grandmother


"People who don't have stories in their cultures go nuts."

—Rafe Martin


"To hunt for symbols in a fairy tale is absolutely fatal."

—W. H. Auden


"Woo the muse of the odd."

—Lafcadio Hearn


"In every generation, children's books mirror the society from which they arise; children always get the books their parents deserve."

—Leonard S. Marcus


"Adults are only obsolete children."

—Dr. Seuss

"I began to realize how simple life could be if one had a regular routine to follow with fixed hours and a fixed salary and very little original thinking to do. The life of a writer is absolute hell compared with the life of a businessman. A person is a fool to become a writer."

—Roald Dahl

"As I look back on what I have written, I can see that the very persons who have taken away my time are those who have given me something to say."

—Katherine Paterson

"Any sufficiently advanced technology is indistinguishable from magic."

—Arthur C. Clarke

"You see, I was one of those people who do not believe in enchantments. And because of that, I must suffer to be enchanted myself, and to be chained and push this millstone around."

—Richard Kennedy, as the Chained Lady,
"Crazy in Love"

"To steal ideas from one person is plagiarism; to steal from many is research."

—A. Felson

"Art is the most intense mode of individualism the world has ever known."

—Oscar Wilde

"Catering to the bored as if they were intellectual invalids only produces a lower and lower threshold of boredom."

—Marilyn Gardner

"That's the trouble with you sad-city types: a place has to be miserable and dull as ditchwater before you believe it's real."

—Salman Rushdie, as Blabbermouth,
*Haroun and the Sea of Stories*

"It's a fair-sized job to write a book that people can be bothered just to read; when they begin to steal copies, you are really getting some place."

—Ruth Stout

"It makes your mind pop."

—Laura Simms

"Telling the proper stories is as if you were approaching the throne of Heaven in a fiery chariot."

—Baal Shem Tov, as quoted by Steve Sanfield

"God made man because he loves stories."

—Rabbi Nachman of Bratzlev, as quoted by
Steve Sanfield

"The destiny of the world is determined less by the battles that are lost and won than by the stories it loves and believes in."

—Harold Goddard, *The Meaning of
Shakespeare*

"Fairy tales are more than true: not because they tell us that dragons exist, but because they tell us that dragons can be beaten."

—G. K. Chesterton

"Australian Aborigines say that the big stories—the stories worth telling and retelling, the ones in which you may find the meaning of your life—are forever stalking the right teller, sniffing and tracking like predators hunting their prey in the bush."

—Robert Moss, *Dreamgates*

"I'm sure there are writers who are great businessmen, but I never met any."

—Arthur Miller

"Words should be weighed, not counted."

—Jewish folk saying

*Also for children's writers . . .*

# THE BUSINESS OF WRITING FOR CHILDREN

## AARON SHEPARD